The Hepburn Chronicles

*Somewhat Off the Mainline
to Way Down East*

*Satire War
and the Corporate Whore*

Remembering Warren Rohrer

The Loons of Holland Pond

Poems by

Andrew Hepburn

The Hepburn Chronicles

Poems by

Andrew Hepburn

Railroad Street Press
St. Johnsbury, Vermont

Copyright (c) 2012 by Andrew Hepburn

All rights reserved

Printed in the United States of America

Photographs and cover design by Andrew Hepburn

Edited by Andrew Hepburn

LIBRARY OF CONGRESS
CATALOGING-IN-PUBLICATION DATA

Hepburn, Andrew.
The Hepburn Chronicles / Andrew Hepburn.

ISBN 9781936711161

Railroad Street Press
394 Railroad St., Ste 2
St. Johnsbury, VT 05819

"Those who have sold their souls are busy
trying to buy them back."
Mark Strand

"You can't corrupt the corrupt."
Kenneth Wilkerson

"Who shall guard the guardians?"
Juvenal

"Satire is born of rage"
Hu Nohs

"Things are more like they are now
than they have ever been."
Dwight D. Eisenhower

"If you can't stand the heat get out of the kitchen."
Harry S. Truman

"Let's get out of the kitchen
before we have to do the dishes."
Louis F. Hepburn

to Paula

*for her tough mind
and warm heart*

to

Jane Rohrer

*for her sharp critiques
and enduring friendship*

and to

my mother and father

for giving us Mountainy Pond

Acknowledgments

Gratitude to Saul Alinsky, Aristophanese, Antonin Artaud, Judith Ashley, Scott and Joelle Beck, Samuel Beckett, Bertolt Brecht, Hayden Carruth, Chris Eaves, Euripides, Michel de Ghelderode, Robert Frost, Jack Germond, Woody Guthrie, Jack Handley, Jennifer Heath, Cabot Hepburn Sayles, Lisa Hepburn, Samuel Hepburn, Shannon Hepburn, Eugene Ionesco, Molly Ivins, Bertram Joseph, Joseph Rosenberg, John Sayles, William Shakespeare, Robert Smith, Mark Strand, Lisa Von Kann and Arne Zaslove.

and special thanks to

David Budbill and Ken Wilkerson

Preface

The elements of theatre inform my poems...they are inescapable...the dynamic nature...the masking...the conflict...the resolution...all conspire to breathe life into the poem...how did I come to this...

Somewhat Off the Main Line to Way Down East:
Born in Bryn Mawr, Pennsylvania, in 1940: I was adrift on the Main Line and adrift at Friends' Central, the Quaker prep School, then less so at Goddard College in Vermont. I studied French Lit because my father said it would be a good thing to do... I said OK... continuing to drift. In my junior year I went to France and attended the Cours de Civilzation Francaise at the Sorbonne in Paris...my junior year adrift... not a bad place to drift. I was perpetually late to class... a colossal lecture hall overflowing with hundreds of foreign students. I would sit in the balcony for a while and as the prof said "Ecrivez, mes eleves, c'est tres important" a sea of heads would bow down. I watched this wave of heads for awhile then left and walked the streets of Paris. Needless to say, "J'ai complement flunkey". However, in my drifting, I saw a lot of French Theatre, maybe thirty-five productions, ranging from Moliere and Racine at the Palais Royale to Genet's The Blacks and the astounding "Bald Soprano" by Ionesco... I was no longer adrift...I was experiencing a strange sensation...having a direction.
I wrote an apprehensive letter to my father and mother saying I wanted to study theatre...please let me do that. My father wrote back and said, "Don't be so apprehensive ...go and study theatre." A great burden was lifted at that moment...a sense of finding oneself...of finding a fix...a navigational fix...a way to move on that had meaning.

Satire War and the Corporate Whore: "It depends whose ox is getting gored"...so said Senator Sam Rayburn about satire. And these days there is alot to gore. To paraphrase Lewis Black, "I took LSD and a shitload of other drugs just to prepare for now!". During my doctoral studies at the U. of Washington, I came to know and learn from Arne Zaslove who made the Commedia DellArte come alive. He passed on to me the teaching of Jaques Lecoq. I made masks such as IL CAPITANO, the incompetent braggart-coward captain of the army and IL PROFESSORE, the professor who knows it all and knows nothing but will profess ad infinitum. So the braggart coward war lovers and those in the know, who know little, and the false piety of the Tartuffes ... these resonate far beyond Zasloves's classroom ...out to today's world.

Remembering Warren Rohrer: During my Main Line drifting years... I met Warren Rohrer who taught the Art History class at Friends' Central. He taught me to see... see closer into things ...to abstract or pull out shapes colors textures...the stuff of the image...he was a teacher and a friend.

The Loons of Holland Pond: During the summer of 2007 I canoed on the pond at daybreak and saw amazing things. Nobody on the pond was awake...it was mine and mine alone...until I saw the Loons... who congregated on the north end of the pond. The poems grew out of these moments. Later I produced a CD, narrating the poems with my daughter, Shannon, which I put to music, with the shakuhachi flute of David Budbill and others... as well as the eerie wonderful calls of the Loons recorded by William Barklow. For copies of this CD, please contact the author directly at ahepburn40@live.com.

The Hepburn Chronicles

Contents

Somewhat Off the Main Line to Way Down East

Main Line Misfit   2
The Main Line.   3
Beyond Between   4
Commencement Terminal   6
Hanging Cock Farm   7
Sassafras   8
Roux   9
Sounds of the Shore   10
Willard   11
Horse Killer   12
A Deep Sadness   13
Planting a Seed   14
Penile Matters   15
The First Call of the Loon   16
Loon Chasing   17
On This Dock.
Close to my Father in Jug Wine Silence   19
Paula   20
Understated Hyperbole   21
Quaker Corral   22
Lost in the Sounds   23
Last Words   24
Passing   25

The Ashes of Our Father   26
Of the Earth   27
Lubec Foggy Dew   28
An Unhinged Door   29
I Fall   30
Persona   31
Mystical Trip   32
A Profound Peace   33
The Intoner   34
Resilience   35
The Big Bed   36
The Wrong Place   37
Wild Bill Arrowsmith   38
Strawberries from Haiti   39
She Hung There   40
Waiting for Godot the Gravedigger   41
Finally My Direct TV Dish is of Some Use   43
Practising for Old Age   44

Satire War and the Corporate Whore

Field Guide to the North American Corporate Whore   46
Spoor   47
Wall Street Awash   48
Gitmo   50
Oil Boarding   51
The Hiss of the Grill   52
The Surge   53
The Stink of War   54
The POW   56
Nation Building   57
Two Limericks for War Lovers   58
Dick and Sarah   59

The Descent   61
Chin On Gut   62
Limericks on Lord Clinton and Saint Newt   63
Embedded with the Kochs   64
The Forbears of Sarah   64
Castraure de San Rush   64
Field Guide to the University Presidential Parrocock   65
SSU Meets Frankie Perdue   66
The Aftermath   67
Retired President For Rent   68
In Search of Itself   69
Never Lose Confidence   70
Buffoons Between God and the Devil   71
The Upper Depths   72
Chicken Pompeii   73
Hanging Offenses Time Place   74
The Mountain with Three Names   75
Good News   76

Remembering Warren Rohrer

Warren Rohrer First Impressions   79
Watching the Woods   81
The First Paintings   83
Transitions Edge   85
Recreating November   87
Warren Rohrer the Other Father   89
Lancaster County Winter   91
Silent Sand Storm   92

The Loons of Holland Pond

The Glacier   94
Holland Pond Home to the Loons   95
Return of the Loons   96
In Mortal Combat for a Mate   97
Birth Watch   98
Out of the Mist   99
Gone   100
Arc into the Sun   101
Summer Storm   102
Dionysiac Loon Dance 1   103
Dionysiac Loon Dance 2   104
Loon Weaving   105
A Matter of Life or Death   106
Departure   107
In My Recurring Dream   108
Convergence of Calls   109

Somewhat Off the Main Line
to Way Down East

Main Line Misfit

was I a Main Line misfit

the Main Line was named I suppose
after the Pennsylvania Railroad line
which runs west from Philadelphia
through upscale locales

born in Bryn Mawr on the Main Line
my name duly entered in the
Philadelphia Social Register
groomed to enter Main Line
and Philadelphia society
attended Junior Dancing Assembly
all of which I dreaded and despised
attended a fine Quaker prep school
somehow barely passing each grade

then I found myself at Goddard College
in the fields and woods of Vermont

I saw the Northern Lights
studied Theatre and married Paula

far from the Main Line

The Main Line

oh you must see this
and you must do this

they had no idea what to do
with their lives
so they told me what to do
with mine

compensatory souls
whose lives were vacuous
sought to appear in the know

this is what I remember
about some who lived
on the Main Line

many of them were well off
no more than well off
and some more than somewhat off

as was I for a time
somewhat off
on the Main Line

Beyond Between

I was there

facing a small man in a big chair
in a tacky office at 69th Street Terminal

between afternoon bus rides from
the Quaker prep school on the Main Line
to the boondocks of West Chester County

I was known as the farm boy
hey Andy did you slop the hogs today

so why there facing a small bald man
it seems I was a train wreck with lousy grades

tell me about yourself he began
with a perfunctory smile

so off I went I know not where
ending with a question
what is beyond the stars

the bald man did not answer
instead he recommended
intense therapy for many years

my parents said no go
and sent me to another shrink

a preppy middle aged man
in a Harris Tweed jacket

he began with a question
regarding my view of myself
in my class at school

where did I stand or fit in
or something like that

after some thought I answered
there are the jocks and the eggheads
and I am somewhere in between

he told my parents that
my answer seemed to be
a rather mature response

so regarding the little man
and the Harris Tweed

that was that

Commencement Terminal

the end seemed near all too near
at my high school commencement

after the address by the distinguished speaker
a small wiry elderly man in a black suit
I found myself directly behind him
as we rose to sing the school anthem he farted

to call it a fart is an understatement
this bodily emanation was loud and long
it seemed interminable as we sang
hail to the blue hail to the grey hail alma mater

it endured as if defying the laws of physics
how on earth could a small man produce this
I was directly behind his behind
thoughts raced through me

his timing was impeccable
he must have been saving it
Roseanna Danner said
Ima gonna die will I survive

finally salvation was at hand
it was not an SBD silent but deadly
it was an LBH loud but harmless

Hanging Cock Farm

perhaps a fitting metaphor for our farm
where I with my mother father and sister
and two younger brothers lived for a time

we were roughly ten miles off the Main Line
on fifteen acres of rolling Pennsylvania hills
in what was then farm country

my father a Philadelphia lawyer once removed
was I guess you would say a gentleman farmer
complete with an old barn pigpen chicken house
turkey cage and roughly ten acres of pasture

he raised two Black Angus but did not fix the fences
they ate the neighbors honeysuckle and tasted of it
he raised a pig or two that grew so big
we could not get them on the truck

he raised chickens then lost interest
and passed the buck on to his sons
I went to college and my brothers took care
of the chickens in a manner of speaking

one large rooster repeatedly attacked them
so they hung the big cock upside down
then ran away only to finally be caught as well

Pop asked why run away because we hung the cock
well where is it now uhh still hanging there
well for Gods sake go cut it down okaaay Pop
and life moved on down on hanging cock farm

Sassafras

Sass I called him
was Choptanks buddy
he was a Chesapeake Bay Retreiver
Choptank was a Black Labrador

when we went to the shore
in Mantoloking New Jersey
Pop took Sass and Choptank to the beach
they would run into the ocean and bite the waves
Pop would have to save the waterlogged dogs

as a boy I would go down the hill with Sass
behind our house in Bryn Mawr
play in the stream and look for muskrats

Sass never wandered very far
when I called him he would always come
looking back I think he was my best friend

he was a big dog with soft curly brown hair
and a gentle kind of sad questioning look

one day Sass disappeared
I looked everywhere
I asked Pop where was Sass

he told me he ate some rat poison
in the neighbors barn
I could not understand it at first

Sass was gone

Roux

we are hiring two colored people
Pop told me when I was maybe five
a young sprout who knew
nothing about colored people

I wandered about our house
trying to envision the people
who looked like colors
of the rainbow how could that be

then Felt and Mary arrived
Felt was a very tall friendly man
with shiny black hair and brown skin
and Mary had black hair too
but lighter brown skin than Felt

she was a cook and her last name
was Lucky or Saucier or something
I learned later she was from New Orleans
and knew how to cook southern things
especially Crab Gumbo

Pop would ask her in a reverent way
Mary could you make a Crab Gumbo
of course Mister Hepburn and she would
lovingly make Gumbo all day long

slowly stroking the huge cast iron pan
she made a deep dark brown roux
Mary told me you make it a dark brown
the roux gives Gumbo a real rich taste

Sounds of the Shore

wind in the tall marsh grasses
small waves of the bay lapping the bulkhead
ocean waves breaking on the beach

I sit on the porch of the summer house
waiting and listening to the sounds
moving around me through me
but waiting most of all for the sound
of the afternoon train

a distant whistle makes me jump up
run across the pebble driveway and wait
nothing save the sound of wind
again the sound of the whistle as the train
moves past the small town of Mantoloking
now the sound of the great steam engine
ever increasing in power

the great black engine finally appears
bellowing smoke sounding like thunder
giant wheels madly driving pistons
sound of steel on steel
volcanic blasts of thick smoke fill the air
it hurtles past me
the engineer waves I wave back

as suddenly as the locomotive comes it goes
boxcar after boxcar finally the caboose
then all fades the train is gone

the wind the waves remain

Willard

was a friendly and energetic
Pekinese
so friendly and energetic

that he would fuck
your foot
when you entered the house

you could count on it
thats what Willard did

he always followed my father
around the farm and garden

my father would come inside
with Willard close behind

one time he entered the house
and slammed the door

on Willards head and
one eye popped out

my father gave him
a new name
Willard the One Eyed Footfucker

one can only wonder
what name
Willard gave my father

Horse Killer

we moved from Bryn Mawr
to a fifteen acre farm
in Newtown Square
somewhat off the Main Line

abutting a substantial
piece of land owned
by Morris Dixon
a noted horse trainer

it was a peaceful place
with rolling hills and
a grove of Locust trees
next to a small pond

however the peace was broken
when one of Morris Dixons
horses was killed and he
accused my mother of the deed

my mother was outraged
I am not a horse killer
but my father was amused
and quietly said to me

who knows son
Philadelphia socialite by day
horse killer by night

A Deep Sadness

as a boy I went with my father down the hill
behind our house with two puppies to
drown them in the pond

knowingly yet unknowingly I went
with my father I cannot remember
who carried them

he threw them into the pond they tried to swim
struggling to survive for a while then
they were gone

in a choked voice my father said I will never
do that again we walked back
up the hill

Planting a Seed

standing at the facing bench
looking out over the Quaker meeting
at the memorial service
for Louie my deceased brother

I told the story of my brother
as a boy he came home from school
and asked my mother

whats fucking
my mother paused then said
its planting a seed

the following day Louie
took a packet of seeds to school
went about the school grounds

and planted them while saying
in a sing song fashion
I am fucking I am fucking

Penile Matters

seated at dinner on a wintery day
with my wife and daughter
son in law and four year old grandson

he asked why my hair was so long
because I am getting bald thats what balding men do
let their hair grow long as I pulled my hair back

he said you look like a bull
do you have a bald penis

be discrete I said to myself and rose from the table
earlier my daughter had counseled discretion
in discussing penile matters with my grandson
she reminded me of a time I had told her about
when I was a young lad at Mountainy Pond in Maine

walking down the hill to the dock naked pulling my penis
my aunt saw me and exclaimed in a brassy voice
dont pull it too hard you will pull it off
so on that evening in Vermont I kept my mouth shut

then the comic muse struck and I had to filter
a remembrance of another time
when my niece in her early teens recited
boys go to Venus to get a big penis

with that in mind I said to my grandson
that rhymes with Venus
and his mind flew to the planets

The First Call of the Loon

I cannot recall
when I first heard
the call of the Loon

but I do recall I was eight years old
perhaps rowing an Old Town boat
on Mountainy Pond in Maine

I was caught by the call

but which one I cannot remember
the wail or the wolf like howl yodel
the maniacal laugh like tremolo

it is a blur but I know I heard a Loon call
it still resonates within me
now that I am seventy one

Loon Chasing

I chased Loons across Mountainy Pond
in our Old Town doubleender rowboat

time and again as a kid in summer on the pond
I would go after the Loons until I was exhausted

trying to predict where it would surface after a long dive
always different never the same its way off there

I would dig one oar in and wheel the boat around
then take off with both oars fast and furious

I tried again and again caught
in the crazy chase of the Loon

laughing at myself when I was so wrong
the Loon surfaced way over there

then once it surfaced right next to me
and looked at me with its red eyes

what a joy for a moment
then it dove once again

On This Dock

she sat naked in the sun
looking up with a quiet smile
on this dock
at the far end of Mountainy Pond
one summer long ago

she sat leaning back
her arms supporting her
with legs extended
with tan shoulders
and white breasts belly and hips
and suntanned legs

she looks up at my father
who in the photo captures
a moment of harmony between them
an all too rare moment

a forced marriage years ago
so she said much later
perhaps coerced into marriage
by her sister and mother
who were charmed and amused by him

yet here on this dock in the sun
a moment of respite
a release from the past
a quiet smile

Close to my Father
in Jug Wine Silence

my father and I sat
on the deck at night
outside our cabin
on Mountainy Pond

all was still

across the pond
the black silhouette
of the far hills
deep blue above

a silence

broken only at times
by a distant call of
the Great Horned Owl

Paula

she did not appear for the first time
walking over the Vermont hill in the sun

nor did I see her for the first time walking
through the corn down by the Winooski river

nothing like that as I recall
she did not get into that

perhaps my first recollection of her
was in the Goddard Learning Aids Center

Goddard College out in the boondocks
of Vermont but boondocks she was not

sitting with tight short skirt and amazing legs
with webbed stockings smoking a cigarette

she watched as I made a French learning aid tape
fumbling my way through reel to reel

it was I who needed the learning aid
and her bemused grin told me she knew it

I was the French teaching assistant
and assistance is what I dearly needed

so watching her watch me screw up the tape
was perhaps the first time she appeared

Understated Hyperbole

my mother in law
was not given
to understatement
she opted for hyperbole

she would say I think Arkansas
should be banned from the USA
this perhaps because her husband
divorced her and married
a lawyer from Arkansas

slut she called her
in an offhand manner

later her husbands wife
passed away and later
still when we met again
my mother in law
turned to me and said

in an understated way
sluts dead

Quaker Corral

he sat most Sundays
in the upper left corner
of the facing benches
in the Quaker meeting

he often spoke of the
value and meaning of
being a birthright Quaker

from his vantage point
he looked over the flock
or perhaps herd of young
well endowed heifers

heifers he called them
and over time
he corralled six of them

Lost in the Sounds

of late afternoon
in Lubec Maine

the sound of the foghorn
in Lubec Narrows

the crow passing
making a strange clucking

the gentle shhhh shhhh
of waves from the Bay of Fundy
stroking the grey sand beach
of Carrying Place Cove

the silence of my lost brother
dead two years but living longer
than I thought possible

the silence of the son
of close friends
lost two weeks ago

Last Words

talking to my Mom as she
was breathing her last breaths
she could not speak but her look
was sharp and focused on me

I talked about Mountainy Pond
where we all went in the summer
a two mile lake called a pond
no electricity just propane kerosene
and wood for light and heat

I talked about the poop scoop
there was no outhouse
just the good old poop scoop
and the woods outback

I talked about fishing for Bass
and hearing the calls of the Loons
about Pop cooking over a wood stove
with a flashlight in his mouth
he called it flashlight cookery

about planting a fairy garden
of Indian Pipes and mushrooms
after a good long rain

it was fun a lot of fun Mom
she looked at me and breathed hard
and nodded slowly yes
I think she heard me

Passing

by the old house on Sugar Hill
we turned back toward the valley

I saw a view I had never seen before
a blue grey sky a bright glow

a light seemed to emanate
from the recess of Franconia Notch

out toward the dark surround
as if the light came from there

and later that day in deep winter
I saw skies I had never seen

waves of irredescent blue
washed over dull grey

a sign perhaps of
my mothers passing

The Ashes of Our Father

have been moved about since he died
some came to rest on my brothers mantle

some traveled to Georgia Maine then St Thomas
and back to Maine with my other brother

and some actually found their way to
the Quaker cemetery family plot
on the Main Line outside Philadelphia

why not scatter what remains of our
fathers remains in the Maine woods

given his gallows humor wish to be
carried naked in a sheet up the hill
behind our cabin on Mountainy Pond
and left for the little varmints to feed on

Of the Earth

the small wooden shed had a bench
did he sleep there I never knew

he was the gardener for my Grandma
she had gardens which went on forever
in Awbury near Germantown

as a young boy I went to the shed
to look for him to talk with him
although he did not talk much

he was tall and thin with grey overalls
and he looked kind of grey all over
like a grey day in Fall

his name was Branch
thats what they called him
just Branch he was tall as a tree

the shed had a hard dark dirt floor
it smelled of the earth and it was

Lubec Foggy Dew

I asked John McGonicle the native Lubecer
what happens when the foggy dew
shuts down the Fourth of July fireworks

ohhh he told me the newcomer oh thats
when there is murder and mayhem
and the next morning they walk the
bloody streets of Lubec looking for bodies

he also told me when the
Lubec foggy dew came in

we sold a T shirt saying
do it in the dew
wet satisfaction
guaranteed

An Unhinged Door

I dream
of an unhinged door
with hinges

floating in space
on a diagonal as I see it
looking down on it on a diagonal

but diagonal in relation to what
floating in space
only my view

a white door floating
in a silver light grey space
immense unending

a four paneled door
with old hinges
it floats

as do I
quiet
still

I Fall

in darkness

the last step gone
or never there

the base missing
a foundation gone

where am I
in the moment

of the fall

Persona

her fingers probe deep within the back of my neck
her hand is hot as she penetrates deeper
the heat radiates through me

I try to continue to play the Mask of Wonder
which I designed some time ago for acting students
but the probing fingers and the wave of heat
are all encompassing and something more

I enter into a state of wonder
becoming the mask
no longer wearing it
but being at one with it
empathy and ecstasy
fuse in the moment
and I am no longer
who I was
but newly created

I whisper
where am I
what is this
then turn to Ilana
and see her
in tears of quiet joy
a shared bliss

she frees me

Mystical Trip

Doc Hep is on a mystical trip
so my students said
at the university

they were right I think
but what did they know
about mystical trips

one did I think
you are Zenning she said
smiling and walked away

my teacher of
Transcendental Meditation
was envious

you are in a state of Satori
no I am not
yes you are

way back in
seventy three
for a time

to rediscover
later perhaps
for a time

A Profound Peace

there is no time in flow
fire is life giving
and life taking
water the same

the gentle mighty opposites
I called them

deadly gamma rays
flow from the sun
transform to life giving rays
which touch the earth

this I came to know somehow
in a mystical moment I believe
I did not study this phenomenon

hmm I think I will have
a mystical experience
and learn of gamma rays
it just happened

I slept very little in this
state of energy flow
I ate little and lost weight

there was a profound peace

The Intoner

the noted poet intoned his words
he was clearly Ivy League
so much so that vines were growing
out of his lower regions

he began his poems
in a sing song fashion
I walked down the Appian Way
and again
I walked down the Appian Way
ad infinitum ad nauseum

sweet Jesus good God deliver me

I left

after the reading I met
a professor of English in the lobby
so Hepburn what did you think

I said after he intoned the words
I walked down the Appian Way
I wanted to interject
thoroughly ensconced in my own profundity

he left

Resilience

our president was a maverick
a pleasant change after all the unctuous types
I had encountered in my wanderings
through the landscape of higher education

I never heard him utter the clichés
the right person for the right job at the right time
or the jewel in the crown and other such rot

after all what president would openly say
to a faculty member oh fuck the faculty
but he did
his name was Bellavance a warlike name
meaning beautiful advance

when he was dying of cancer
I asked him in his office
about his favorite Frost poem

he answered The Birches in Winter
young Birch trees bow down in winter snow
then afterward they spring back up

as we talked a young student came to
his office door asking him for an interview
but you just interviewed me she stood there

I tell you what I will let you know when I am dead
she stared at him then left as he laughed quietly

The Big Bed

the new college student enters
his dorm room for the first time
and sees a young black student

they exchange greetings
the white student eyes the room
and the black student eyes him

could you get my trunk downstairs
the white student asks
a gasp from students watching
the improv in the theatre class

I am not the custodian
the black student replies
I am your roommate

oh says the white student
who pauses then tosses his suitcase
on the larger bed of the two

thats my bed the black student says
the white student looks at him
why is it your bed

the black student answers
big dick big bed

the class explodes with laughter

The Wrong Place

I tape the leaky front door of our house
an interior door used for the front door
a door wrongly placed

am I wrongly placed I wonder
here again in Vermont
on a hard winters day with wind howling
as the temperature soars to zero

years before Paula and I lived as newlyweds
in a rented room of a house poised
to fall into the Winooski River
the walls did not quite meet the floors
and little snow drifts blocked the wind

but now I feel trapped in my own house
by the painters tape I used on the exit

so I escape through the garage door
to the Pope Memorial Library in Danville
where a loud avalanche of snow slides off
the roof and traps me in the Pope

so once again I ask
am I in the wrong place
no I am simply coming home

Wild Bill Arrowsmith

we walk along a beach at Marthas Vineyard
the noted classicist William Arrowsmith and I

I ask him about daemons and the daemonic
he answers it was a daemon that led Oedipus to his
wife mother Jocasta where he finds her dead then
takes her broaches and dashes his eyes out

as we continue along the beach
gulls and terns appear in ever greater numbers
in a fury of shrill cries they dive at us

what the Hell is going on I ask
he answers we are intruding on their nesting place
as a large gull dives at our heads

Jesus Christ why did you take me here
he laughs a wild laugh and walks on
through the diving gulls and terns

Strawberries from Haiti

told by William Arrowsmith

a small Greenwich Village
restaurant in the 1960s

enter a genteel woman a kind of
Blanche Dubois does New York
she sits at a small table
enter the brusque owner a kind of
New York version of Stanley Kowalski

what can I get you lady
I would like some strawberries please

he returns shortly with the strawberries
are these strawberries from Haiti
listen lady what do you care
where they come from

well I understand the Haitians have Aids
so I just wondered
listen lady they pick the strawberries
they dont fuck em

She Hung There

from the low branch
with siren smile
silently calling
come take me
take me down

we had left the rest of
our high school class
and walked to the
other side of the farm

I went ahead thinking
she was right behind
then turned to see her
just hanging there
with long brown hair
down to her waist

I stood there still
just staring at her
at some distance
from the tree
silently standing

Waiting for Godot the Grave Digger

hello dolly I said to the dolly
bearing my mothers gravestone
as I pushed it up the gentle slope
past the Quaker meeting house
to the small cemetery beyond
not really but I thought of saying it

we had waited for the gravedigger
however like Godot he never showed
and so we were there on a raw March day
with the wind swirling wildly about us
we were there to bury my mother

as we trudged up the hill like Didi and Gogo
my wife behind me with Marions ashes
I became Lear howling blow winds
and crack your cheeks and grabbing
my mothers ashes and casting them
into the wind about the cemetery
but I did not do that I just pushed on

but how did I know to bring a dolly
because this was deja vu all over again
a repeat of an earlier scene
some years before when I came
to bury my brother in which Godot
the gravedigger never showed

My Direct TV dish is finally of some use!

Finally my Direct TV Dish is of Some Use

I was pissed off at the CEO of Direct TV

of course Mr Hepburn you can receive all
the major networks when we install your dish
however this proved not to be the case

consistent lie upon lie so I drop kicked
Direct TV through the goal posts of life

but I was stuck with their fucking dish
on the roof of my house to be removed
at my expense the CEO did not want it

and I was stuck in a whirlpool of revenge
going nowhere fast in my disgust
until the muse struck which one I am not sure

I created a fountain with a cherubic figure
which pissed off my wife but left me ecstatic

with a quiet joy it transported me back in time
to an ancient garden in a Tuscan Villa

and in the late afternoon sun the
cherubic figure had a contemplative look
as it quietly urinated into the Direct TV Dish

Practicing for Old Age

I drove halfway
to Danville with my
right turn signal on

in the drugstore as
I left the pharmacist
I said Hi

Satire War
and the Corporate Whore

A Field Guide to the North American Corporate Whore
avis corporatus prostitutus

a large predatory fowl with
white head and multicolored hair
white neck although red at times
often sharp eyed however at times
having a benign appearance with
grey plumage and gold accessories

often sighted on golf courses
throughout North America and migrates
to southern golf courses in winter
although flocks of Corporate Whores
have been sighted around the oil rich
countries of the Middle East and Africa
breeds in gated communities from
Canada to southern parts of USA
breeding grounds are clean and pristine
while befouling the rest of the land
it preys on just about anything

whereas nature abhors a vacuum
the Corporate Whore loves it
attracted to fiscal vacuums
it can at times be seen flying
into fiscal black holes where
it disappears in cosmic suck

in flight it cries I am poor I am poor
and extremely vocal on ground
the Corporate Whore rarely shuts up

Spoor

lets out and find some peasant spoor
its always fun to hunt the poor

a friend of my fathers
created this rhyme
a long time ago
on a hunting trip
in the Maine woods

it stayed with me
for some reason
and years later
I revised the rhyme

lets out and find some CEO spoor
its fun to hunt the corporate whore

Wall Street Awash

and it came to pass
that the citizenry was pissed off
pissed off with Wall Street

they were so pissed off
that they pissed Wall Street offshore
down the Hudson and out into the Atlantic

the force of the great flood tide of urine
devastated the lower end of the island
and Wall Street was gone

there were no streets left and no walls
only the residue of what was

the corporate whores were gone
the executive suites as well
and the high priced troughs where they fed

so too the country clubs where they played
these their fairways and greens
became one tan and shit brindle

the masks of the virtuous benefactors
were violently washed away
torn off by the force of the piss

revealing at the moment of their demise
the face of the Semper Fide
or fuck you Jack I've got mine

washed out to sea amidst a great band
of Wall Street flotsam and jetsam
becoming a long island of detritus

amidst the debris was a sign which read
Venite Porcelli e Gustate a Corporatum Patinam
o come ye swine and feed at the corporate trough

some literati said Rabelais would be amused
and Gargantua pissed that he was not invited

some said God said it was good
some just said holy shit

Gitmo

Keep Gitmo Open for
the corporate whores
was the resounding
cry across the land

and lo it came to pass
the corporati prostituti
were tried and found guilty
for a raft of crimes
against the citizenry

such things as
corporate manslaughter
corporate fraud and other
crimes against humanity

a few were hung on
the Capitol Mall but
Dick Cheney was spared
and sent to Gitmo to

become the Gitmo Greeter
it proved difficult for him
instead of have a nice day
it was go and fuck yourself

Oil Boarding

it went on and on

the befouling of the waters off the coasts
until the people rose up and
brought down the corporate whores
responsible for the befouling

they tied them to rakes and dragged them
along the oil soaked beaches
to use them to clean the shores
down in the oil soaked sand

the power elite cried out how dare you
how dare you engage in such barbaric practices

come have some Texas Tea was the reply
come have some Black Gold before you die

alongside the Brown Pelican now black
alongside the workers on the rigs

Hiss of the Grill

slab of meat slapped on
hot metal

sound of improvised explosive device
tearing of flesh and bone
torn apart

sound of wine poured into glass
crack of lobster shell about to be
consumed

cries of agony and grief and loss
mingled with sounds of
public prayer

strains of Home on the Range
waft over the Briary
on the Chesapeake Bay

sounds of Abu Grahib
hiss of the grill

The Surge

let those in high office
who propose the surge

those who order the surge
those who support the surge
who have the public trust

let them lead the surge
like Alexander the Great

and perhaps like the
soldiers in the line of fire
moving on roads laden with
improvised explosive devices

perhaps like so many
non fighting men women
and children

be mutilated or blown
to kingdom come

The Stink of War

I could smell it
almost I think

as I walked across the campus
of the University of Washington
on a Spring day in May 1970

the putrid foul stench of napalm
burning human flesh in Vietnam

but I had never smelled that
I only sensed that I was smelling it

years later I smelled the putrid odor
of the Purdue chicken rendering plant
in downtown Salisbury Maryland
was it somewhat the same

the stink of the students killed
at Kent State University
and Nixon saying
in so many words
they deserved it

I went on strike
as a graduate teaching assistant
in the School of Drama
and I think I was the only
one in that school who did

as for the other Theatre students
whats the difference between
ignorance and apathy
I dont know and I dont care

I joined the protest parade
in Seattle and took photos
of Moms Against the War
skinheads with signs SDS Sucks

and a poster of Nixon
looking as if someone had
turned on a vacuum cleaner
and shoved it up his ass

and on and on
the stink of war

The POW

was nameless

Charlie my father
and his Jewish friend Paul
were GI guards in a POW compound
in Aachen Germany during WWII

on a quiet afternoon in the compound
Charlie and Paul were sipping cognac

the peace was broken by a cry
and a blur of a body falling past
their window to the cement below

in the quiet moment that followed
Paul slowly turned and looked
at Charlie and muttered

Superman

Nation Building

it has been learned
from official sources that the
Bush Cheney White House had a covert plan

to annex the oil rich parts of the Middle East and
create a new nation encompassing the oil fields of
Iraq Iran Saudi Arabia Kazakhstan etcetera etcetera

the new nation was to be called
the Federated Union of Corporate Kings
or FUCK for short

word has it that former Vice President Cheney
planned to be the President of the University
of the Federated Union of Corporate Kings

which has led to speculation
about its popular name
FUCK U

Limericks for War Lovers

Crab Rummy

woe betide Lord Rumsfeld the great
who met a most gastronomical fate
he abandoned the war retired to the shore
was dismembered and rendered crab bait

Pene Alla Griglia

to be the Baghdad Messiah
was Cheneys greatest desiah
but alas instead it was off with his head
and they grilled his dick in the fiah

Dick and Sarah

look look oh look see Sarah hunt
see Sarah hunt with Dick

look look see Dick
see Dick take Sarah hunting

see Sarah spy a pheasant
see Sarah fire her gun into the sun

uh oh look look
see Sarah shoot Dicks head off

uh oh look look see Dick walk
see Dick walk without a head

uh oh he never did that before

"American Idle"
G W Bush as SUV
sculpture by
Lisa Hepburn

The Descent

and lo it came to pass
Dante took one look
at George and Dick
and said come on down

they passed with trepidation
through Hellmouth
and began the long descent
into the bowels of Inferno

what circle of Hell is unclear
but it took some time until
they found themselves walking
in the great Mare de Cacca

they proceeded slowly
with heads held high
it was a necessity to keep
their chins above sea level

Jesus Dick said George
this smells like shit
it is shit you idiot

Chin on Gut

sitting there
on TV with his chin
resting on his great gut

Henry Kissinger
was selling his book
On China on Colbert

like some kind of geriatric
No Neck Monster out of
Cat on a Hot Tin Roof

or the fifth face etched
on Mount Rushmore with
a distended bulge beneath

Henry faced Steven with
his great gut under his chin
discussing China under Mao

Mao killed untold thousands
of his own people said Colbert
that may be said Henry

but business is business
said Henry with a casual
wave of his hand

Limericks on
Lord Clinton
and Saint Newt

Clinton the Contrite

Lord Clinton attempted redemption
by donning the mask of contrition
then he sighed what the fuck
his dick ran amuck
and contrition turned to coition

Newts Fruit

woe betide the great Saint Newt
caught under Sunnunus boot
despite outraged calls
John chainsawed his balls
and hung them just like strange fruit

Embedded with the Kochs
or
Get Over It and Get In

the Kochs have a bed like a bin
laden with rank kith and kin
but throw back the cover
and move over Grover
Justice Scalia wants in

The Forbears of Sarah

they walked side by side on the terra
T Rex and the forbears of Sarah
for when alls said and done
they were a family of one
in the great Palinlithic era

Castraure de San Rush
or
The Strange Fate of Limbaugh's Balls

his cohones were found by some cats
and preserved in formaldehyde vats
finally Lisa Kudrow
confessed to his woe
and she practised by castrating rats

A Field Guide
to the University
Presidential Parrocock
avis deviatis parrocockus

Description   a cross between a Parrot and a Peacock
the Parrocock is a deviant species   it is adept at camouflage
and appears benign but can be deadly
Peacock like behavior can be seen in the Fall and Spring
strutting with full plumage usually at the front of a flock of
avis facultatis and other wannabe Parrococks

Habitat   Parrococks prefer manicured surroundings
and breed in well groomed nests near the university
upon migrating to a new habitat Parrococks typically claim
they hit the ground running then vigorously
delegate work to other aspiring Parrococks

Calls   Parrot like calls are extremely repetitive such as
family vision   tansparency   as well as   crown jewel
as if mimicking other Parrococks   Peacock sounding cries
of alarm can be piercing and unpleasant when the big bird is
under attack or believes it is being threatened

the Parrocock is not an endangered species

SSU Meets Frankie Purdue

there was a glitch in the gift to be given
by Frankie Purdue to our university
to endow a School of Business at SSU

it came to the attention of the Ronald Reagan Commission
on Organized Crime that
Frankie Perdue had consulted with
the Castellano crime family in NYC

to come to Accomack Virginia and bust heads
to break up an effort to unionize the workers
at his Purdue chicken processing plant

the esteemed Senate members of RRCOC
asked Frankie Perdue if this was true
and Mr Perdue said yes thats true

somewhat stunned the senators asked
what did the Castellano family say

they asked where is Accomack Virginia
I told them it was on the Eastern Shore
of Virginia south of New Jersey

they said that was out of their territory

that was that except for the gift
so what did SSU do just let it be cool
for a time and delay the birth of the School

and a secretary who worked in that School
was told by a prof oh so cool
watch your knees

Aftermath

the response to the incident
was nothing short of zero
as if one was subjected to Kafkas
mysterious machine without
the meticulous cutting into flesh

a senior professor of English said
Frank Perdue did nothing wrong
and all the students I questioned
said I dont know and I dont care
in other words whats the difference
between ignorance and apathy

but one business student gave
me a response so complex and
morally contorted that I felt I was
being subjected to Kafkas machine
and the rest didnt give a shit

however a professor whose father
had a restaurant in Boston said Andy
you cant escape it its there like air
and as I walked away in disgust
he said youre still my friend arent you

so I told my students prostitution
comes in many forms it involves
compromising your moral principles
for power money or prestige

one student asked what if they had
no moral principles to begin with
now that is a good question

Retired President
For Rent

recently retired president of esteemed
major university in New England

can articulate vision plans at will
can do just about anything even teach

no longer wears the effete presidential mask
noted scholar poet and a real down home guy

capable of wiping off the unctuous
patronizing grin at times

brain in top condition barely used

just $350,000 a year a real deal
yes thats only $350,000 a year

In Search of Itself

why asked the university student
why so much money

it is a good investment
replied the university president
when challenged by the student

but why pay three hundred and
fifty thousand dollars for a dean
why is it a good investment

left unsaid was the following
so the dean can raise more money
and hire more top flight faculty
and pay them more money as well

yet another instance of
money in search of itself

Never Lose Confidence

I was once witness to a lively exchange
twixt two professors who chanced to meet
in the hallowed halls of the university

one a tall bearded imposing man in a dark suit
the other a tall bearded imposing man in a tweed jacket

the dark suit raved about the film Manon of the Spring
it is like a Greek tragedy I could praise it to the skies
the tweed squared off and said as only you can

by God said the dark suit
I would like to cut off your balls
they would grow back replied the tweed

and that was about it except that
neither professor recalled the exchange

it took me back to a time when my father
full of food and drink
would say about his erring sons

never lose confidence in your sons
and my mind echoed
never lose confidence in higher education

Buffoons Between God
and the Devil

we were deformed and contorted
some thirty of us students in the
class on buffoons taught by Lecoq

in our deformed states we mocked
we played at everything always
misshapen and grotesque we were the
buffoons between god and the devil

Jacques Lecoq told us of the lepers of old
outcast from town in their own colony
and once a year they were brought
into town to purge and to cleanse

and on this occasion the lepers would
in their deformities parade through
the town and mock the good people
the bankers the lawyers and such
playing at and saying I am the banker

and still the buffoon show continues but
now the outcasts are in and we the people
fools that we are we watch the parade
of the incast investors and bankers

in their deformities and contortions
as they march past us and through us
playing at freedom and country and on
to somewhere between god and the devil

The Upper Depths

it came to pass
the last college on Earth
was underground
the surface of the
Earth was unfit to live on

the last institution of higher learning was
down in the depths hence the upper depths

the college was located in the Art department digs
the old subterranean boiler room of the college

after untold wars and befouling of the earth
the only department space that remained
was Art because Art did not matter

but Art was annexed by English History
Math Philosophy Foreign Languages
High Energy Physics and Business

the faculty met regularly in the old boiler room
to consider and debate short and long range plans

there were no students but this did not deter
the faculty from their appointed rounds

why no students
it was rumored that due
to a sparse food supply
the faculty ate them

Chicken Pompeii

I first experienced this
gastronomical oddity in
the University Dining Hall
during Secretaries Day
I ate it or some of it then
wondered how was this created
it finally came to me
you take a chicken breast
dip it in egg wash then
bread it and fry it
then bury it at the
foot of Mount Vesuvius
for two thousand years
then disinter reheat and serve
and that is Chicken Pompeii

Hanging Offenses Time Place

1930 Indiana
lynching of two black men falsely accused
then a poem and later a song sung in 1939
by Billie Holiday called Strange Fruit

1959 Vermont
Goddard College President Pitkin who spoke
on his approach to the educational process
I give students enough rope to hang themselves

1967 New Hampshire
the skinny farmer with a huge goiter told me of
the last public hanging in New Hampshire
we were on the way when a horse and carriage
passed us and and a man stuck his head out and said
take it easy boys the show wont start until I get there

1978 Pennsylvania
my father was against Capitol Punishment
however he did think at times that a
public hanging of a white collar crook
would have a salutary effect on the country

2011 Vermont
the gal in the deli thought it was funny
how can you tell if a nigger is well hung
simple if you cant get your finger
between the rope and his neck

time place
on and on

The Mountain with Three Names

the mountain had no name
when it was
forged by earth forces

later it was called Six Grandfathers by Lakota Sioux
or WakanTanka
the unknown universe and unknowable force of life

but the mountain was left alone

and later it was named Mount Rushmore
in honor of a lawyer
from New York named Rushmore

but the mountain was left untouched

still later an historian from South Dakota hired
a sculptor to carve the faces
of four presidents into Mount Rushmore

and it became a tourist attraction

and later still a Lakota Sioux artist painted a picture
and named it
Four Ways to Fuck Up A Mountain

Good News

as a species
we are embarked

on a path of
self destruction

the good news is
I will be dead

Remembering Warren Rohrer

Warren Rohrer
in his Studio

Philadelphia
Pennsylvania

Warren Rohrer
First Impressions

he was the incarnation of opposites
as he walked around us
lecturing on art masters
in Europe and America

we sat there in silence
a senior class in art history
at the Quaker school on the
Main Line of Philadelphia

we sat there looking at slides
and rarely asking questions
as he moved slowly around
like some kind of god

with a deep resonant voice
he spoke about paintings
or sculpture by Michelangelo
to the Hudson River School

strolling around the
perimeter of the class
he was august remote
yet kind and friendly

and amused at times
by our responses
which he revealed
with a quiet smile

time passed and I began
to talk with him
one on one in his office

we were drawn to nature
and its changes
as the seasons passed

at years end he gave the
class two pieces of advice
his first piece of advice
was take no advice and

the second piece of advice
there is no risk in taking a risk
but there is all the risk
in the world in taking no risk

time passed and I visited his place
in Lancaster County
and met his wife Jane
who wrote poems that I loved
but strangely did not understand

I gave Warren a mobile of
cut glass with varied colors
he hung it in his studio in the barn

it moved as did our friendship
to something indefinable yet enduring

Watching the Woods

we sat in silence
for the most part

looking out over
the high school
soccer and football fields
at the woods beyond

we sat in his office
Warren Rohrer
my art teacher and I

we watched the woods
turn over time
from Spring to Fall

colors textures shapes
in the morning light
we watched the changes

Edges
like an early Rohrer

Schoodic Point
Maine

The First Paintings

I saw by Warren Rohrer
were small in scale but thick with pigment

oil paintings layer upon layer
applied with a palette knife

in such a way that the edges of each shape
pushed against the previous layer of pigment

thereby concealing the former layer but
revealing hints of it around the edges

it was the rich thick pigment and
the edge which caught me

a struggle to stop or wipe out or
merge with the previous edge

like a time in ones life
that blots out previous time
almost but not quite

that is what caught me
at the time and still does

Water Meets Granite

The Basin
Franconia Notch
New Hampshire

Transitions Edge

where the prairie meets
the mountains approaching
Glacier National Park

where the cliffs edge falls
to Birch and boulders below
on Mountainy Pond in Maine

where water meets granite
at the Basin near the source
of the Pemigewasset River

where ice meets water
on the shore of
Holland Pond in April

where the soy bean field
meets the woods near
Salisbury Maryland

where the high school
sports field meets the woods
on the Main Line

where land meets sea
on the Bay of Fundy
near Lubec Maine

I stop and wonder

Remembering 9-11

Cobscook Bay
Lubec, Maine

Recreating November

is a pencil sketch I made

to rediscover an oil painting
by Warren Rohrer created years ago
which he called November

it stopped me I could not
move on about the gallery to
view the rest of his work

brooding haunting
greys within greys
quiet formal edges

deep resonating infinities
within the edges
that took me away like the tide

a grey window to
the great beyond

Jane Rohrer told me
Warren never painted
such a work

and so it is a mystery

Morning Light

Bay of Fundy
Maine

Warren Rohrer
the Other Father

he was the other father for
mine I felt was missing
at times

although I think I was closer
to him than my sister and
two brothers

I was distant apart from him
my father

so there was this other
father

Water and Light on Granite

The Basin
Franconia Notch
New Hampshire

Lancaster County Winter

two crows flying through
a gray winter sky over
fields of wheat and snow

Silent Sand Storm

from miles above the
earth a sandstorm is
silent as is the water of
Holland Pond brushed
by an evening wind

in late summer cones
of sandlike particles
move in gentle slant
toward the far hills

converging near the
rock strewn shore
separated only by a
bronze bar of still water
reflecting the trees
beginning to turn

The Loons of Holland Pond

The Glacier

moves

it appears still and lifeless
yet the massive body of ice
is a creative force of nature
sculpting rock formations
which surround it

it moves

gravity and manifold layers
of impacted snow
reform the ice into an
interlocking pattern of ice crystals
wrenching great hunks of rock
from their bases

the glacier grinds polishes and erodes
as it inches forward
it splits into giant crevasses
hundreds of feet deep
as earth forces act upon it
the glacier throws up pulverized rock

over time it creates and shapes
what much later
comes to be called

Holland Pond

Holland Pond
Home to the Loons

roughly fifty springs
feed the body of water
called Holland Pond

lying at the foot of mount Barnston
the one and a half mile pond is in
the far northern part of Vermont
little more than a stones throw
from the Canadian border

forty cabins line the western shore
but the eastern shore is wild

home to the Loons

Return of the Loons

Spring thaw
the ice is out and once again
one can hear the call of the Loon

wintering along the New England coast
and other bodies of water well to the South
the Loons return to Holland Pond
to create a new generation

my summer neighbor the Loon man
hauls two floating docks out on the pond
and anchors them offshore as safer sites
for the Loons to build their nests

the Loon man is a witness
and keeper of the Loons

In Mortal Combat for a Mate

a Loon chases another Loon
across Holland Pond

wings and webbed feet
beating water propelling
each one forward at great speed

the pursuer catches the pursued
the chase ends the fight begins

the Loon drives his bill into
the breast of the other Loon
then grabs his throat with his bill

pulls him down under the water to his death
while the mate dives for minnows

Birth Watch

two speckled eggs
lie in the Loons nest
on Holland Pond

usually vulnerable to predators
like the skunk mink or raccoon
these eggs are somewhat safer

the Loon man has anchored
a floating dock offshore
away from the predators

the Loons use this safer site to
make a nest and incubate
the eggs for two weeks or so

chirping before they
break through the shell
the chicks are born

the Loon man watches
through his telescope
from the near shore

and atop a giant spruce tree
from the far shore
the Bald Eagle watches

Out of the Mist

moving through mist at dawn
canoe slicing through water

a dark figure emerges
out of the mist a Loon

directly ahead moving
toward me its round
black head like a torpedo

I freeze and watch as it
moves silently past me

then is gone into the mist

Gone

Spring on Holland Pond

two Loon chicks follow
in their mothers wake

a Bald Eagle watches
atop a giant Spruce
on the far shore

the Eagle leaves his perch
and flies toward the Loons
circling above them

the mother Loon
hastens toward the shore
with her chicks

the Eagle dives
dropping fast

with talons extended
it plucks a Loon chick
from the pond

the Eagle flies back
to the giant Spruce
with its prey

Arc into the Sun

as I canoe at dawn on Holland Pond
I ponder my mothers life slipping away

a Loon flies along the far shore
then circles toward me
around the north end of the pond

it disappears behind tall spruce
only to suddenly reappear directly
over me with sound of beating wings
like a steam engine in the distance

as I turn my canoe to follow its path
it makes another arc
this time toward the morning sun
and disappears in the light

looking left and right
no sign of the Loon

I return to the image of the Cormorant
I saw earlier in the summer
flying in an arc over Cobscook Bay
and like the Loon disappearing in the sun

I wonder is this another sign
of my mother her life lived
and now moving on

Summer Storm

a storm approaches
on Holland Pond

distant thunder then silence
clouds race across the pond

a Loon calls

wind gusts as the sky
turns dark blue grey
thunder is potent and near

no sound of the Loon

lightning bolts across the pond
hard rain strikes the water
like giant waves

then subsides
trees which were thrown about
are still

in the calm a Loon calls

Dionysiac Loon Dance 1

amidst a cluster of Loons
one Loon suddenly
flies across the pond

erect on the water
standing straight up
streaking across the pond

with bill thrust down
neck arched up and back
breast undulating forward

like a fluid sinuous S
racing across the water
engaged in a
wild balancing act

the black Loon tears
across the surface
of the gold shining pond

like a Dionysiac vision
for his mate

Dionysiac Loon Dance 2

dawn in late summer on Holland Pond
three Loons are in a line on the water

nothing moves

suddenly two Loons on either side
explode in opposite directions
wings furiously beating on water

they seem to fly on the surface
racing madly some fifty yards
out away from the center Loon

who remains still

as suddenly as they began
both Loons simultaneously stop

and together as in a formal dance
they turn and slowly glide
back to the center Loon

who remains still

Loon Weaving

a placid dawn
seven Loons converge
in an informal way

then quietly form a
line like a parade
and swim slowly
across the pond

the lead Loon turns and
weaves back and forth
through the line

as do each of the
following Loons
weaving in turn
like a braid

in what seems
an ancient rite
of late summer

A Matter of Life or Death

Autumn approaches

and the young Loon must learn
to fly or be frozen in the
snow and ice of Holland Pond

he practices

surging forward with
webbed feet and wings
furiously propelling him
for three hundred yards

to no avail he must try again

after each attempt he swims back
to the opposite end of the pond
to face into the wind

the wind picks up and
as it does the young Loon
once again runs across the water

and flies

Departure

the young Loon flies in
a great circle to gain altitude
then heads East toward the
coastal waters of New England

leaving Holland Pond
to return in the Spring
the pond is still
a long deep silence

save for the sound
of water flowing
into Holland Brook

which flows West to
join the Tomifobia River
then the Saint Francois

to merge with the waters of
the Saint Lawrence River
and the Gulf of Saint Lawrence

where fresh and salt waters
merge and move on to
the majestic North Atlantic

In My Recurring Dream

I am pulled overboard
into the ocean caught in
the net I use to catch fish

pulled down ever deeper
I tear wildly to
extricate myself

in vain I drown
in my own net

so goes my
recurring dream

so goes the recurring
experience of the Loon

while diving for fish
it is caught in the purse seine
and drowns in the great net
of the giant factory boat

the Loon is dragged on deck
with the catch of the day
then tossed overboard
into the North Atlantic

but this is no dream

Convergence of Calls

a still dark night
on Holland Pond

two Loons sound the laughing call
rapid statement and response
a frenzied back and forth
the calls build to a climax

then silence

from the south a third Loon calls
a long plaintive wail
a high lonesome bluegrass call
like a wolf howl

silence

then an eruption of sound
all call in quick succession
and the mountain echoes
as if calling back
to the Loons

sounds resonate
down the far hills
of Holland Pond

About the Poet

Andrew Hepburn holds a B.A in theatre from Goddard College, an M.A. in theatre from Northwestern University and a Ph.D. in drama from the University of Washington.

1970: designed masks of the Commedia Dell'Arte for productions by Arne Zaslove and Actor Training at the University of Washington.

1976: designed Commedia masks for production of "The Servant of Two Masters" by Goldoni

produced at University of Houston-Victoria Campus 1977: designed masks for Euripides, "The Bacchae" produced at Marquette University

1970s to present: wrote poetry, Haiku and limericks

1980: translated "The King Stag" by Carlo Gozzi with Dr. Carozza, which he directed at Marquette University.

1984: wrote a screenplay, "Pristine Condition" on the theme of self-destruction and in 1986, wrote "The Upper Depths or the Last College on Earth"

1999: founded Art Culture Nature, a national organization for the study of the Arts and the Environment.

2007: wrote "The Loons of Holland Pond" and produced a CD of the poems with music and Loon calls.

Acted in university and professional theatres including Champlain Shakespeare Festival, ACT in Seattle and the Milwaukee Repertory Theatre. Directed and designed university productions.

Andrew may be contacted directly at ahepburn40@live.com

www.ingramcontent.com/pod-product-compliance
Lightning Source LLC
Chambersburg PA
CBHW061447040426
42450CB00007B/1256